Extreme
ULTRA
RUNNING

Virginia Loh-Hagan

45th Parallel Press

Published in the United States of America by Cherry Lake Publishing
Ann Arbor, Michigan
www.cherrylakepublishing.com

Content Adviser: Liv Williams, Editor, www.iLivExtreme.com
Reading Adviser: Marla Conn, ReadAbility, Inc.
Photo Credits: ©Greg Epperson/Shutterstock.com, cover, 1; ©Simon Maycock/Alamy Stock Photo, 5; ©Maridav/Shutterstock.com, 6; ©Klemen Misic/Shutterstock.com, 8; ©Pete Saloutos/Shutterstock.com, 11; ©Klemen Misic/Shutterstock.com, 13; ©Bikeworldtravel/Shutterstock.com, 15; ©Aurora Photos/Alamy Stock Photo, 17; ©Hdsidesign/Dreamstime.com, 19; ©Klemen Misic/shutterstock.com, 21; ©Brian A Jackson/Shutterstock.com, 23; ©Marcos Ferro/Aurora Photos/Aurora Photos/Corbis, 25; ©Yannis Kontos/Polaris/Newscom, 26; ©Maridav/shutterstock.com, 29; ©Trusjom/Shutterstock.com, multiple interior pages; ©Kues/Shutterstock.com, multiple interior pages

45th Parallel Press is an imprint of Cherry Lake Publishing.

Library of Congress Cataloging-in-Publication Data

Names: Loh-Hagan, Virginia.
Title: Extreme ultra running / by Virginia Loh-Hagan.
Description: Ann Arbor : Cherry Lake Publishing, [2016] | Series: Nailed it!
  | Includes bibliographical references and index.
Identifiers: LCCN 2015026817| ISBN 9781634704847 (hardcover) | ISBN
  9781634705448 (pdf) | ISBN 9781634706049 (paperback) | ISBN 9781634706643
  (ebook)
Subjects: LCSH: Marathon running--Juvenile literature. | Extreme
  sports--Juvenile literature. | ESPN X-Games--Juvenile literature.
Classification: LCC GV1065 .L65 2016 | DDC 796.42/52--dc23
LC record available at http://lccn.loc.gov/2015026817

ABOUT THE AUTHOR

Dr. Virginia Loh-Hagan is an author, university professor, former classroom teacher, and curriculum designer. Walking to her mailbox is enough exercise for her! Sometimes, she naps along the way. She lives in San Diego with her very tall husband and very naughty dogs. To learn more about her, visit www.virginialoh.com.

Table of Contents

To the Finish Line!

What is a marathon? What is an ultra runner? Who is Kevin Carr? Who is James Tufnell? Who is Scott Jurek?

A **marathon** is a footrace. It's 26.2 miles (42 kilometers). Imagine running even farther. That's what **ultra runners** do. They really run long distances.

Kevin Carr ran about 31 miles (50 km) a day. He ran for 621 days. He ran a total of 16,299 miles (26,231 km). He took 36 million steps. He ran around the world. He ran through deserts. He suffered from heat and sand. He ran around the North Pole. He faced harsh **arctic** weather. Arctic refers to cold weather. He ran up mountains. He had difficulty breathing.

He avoided snakes, wolves, and mountain lions. He saw 26 bears in five weeks. One bear followed him. Carr had many problems. But he overcame them. He said, "I'm overwhelmed. It was an amazing finish."

James Tufnell competed in a 155-mile (249.5 km) race. After running 50 miles (80.5 km), he ran down a sand hill.

Ultra runners travel the world. Kevin Carr ran across Europe, India, Australia, New Zealand, North America, South America, and Ireland.

Ultra runners learn how to endure. They don't quit.

A rock trapped his leg. He smashed his ankle. He broke his leg. But he kept going for the last 100 miles (161 km). He faced the heat. He had to carry his own supplies. His supplies included food, water, and sleeping gear.

Tufnell said, "I remember stumbling and swearing a lot. But I didn't fall." He almost gave up. But a camel chased him to the finish line. He finished with 10 minutes left in the race.

Scott Jurek has won many awards in ultra running. He's been called the top ultra runner in the world. He's very

Advice from the Field: Rory Bosio

Rory Bosio is an ultra runner. She won the North Face Ultra Trail du Mont Blanc. This is a 103-mile (165.7 km) race. She climbed 31,000 feet (9,449 meters). She did it in less than 23 hours. She started running in her teens. She runs up to 100 miles a week. Her body suffers from this running. She advises doing yoga at least 15 minutes a day. She said, "It's all too easy to focus on how much I'm suffering during the low points of an ultra. Chafing, blisters, cramps, and just plain exhaustion are common obstacles during any endurance event. However, through yoga I've learned to center my mind and concentrate on my breathing. ...I'm able to focus on all the fabulous parts of ultra running: the amazing people I meet, the scenery, and the sense of accomplishment that comes after you've run more in one day than most people do in a month!"

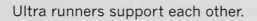

Ultra runners support each other.

excited about racing. He screams loudly at the beginning of races. He rolls over finish lines. He does kung fu leaps into **aid stations**. Aid stations are checkpoints. They provide runners with water, snacks, and help.

He usually finishes races in the top places. But he stays for hours. He cheers other runners. Ultra runners respect their sport. They run as individuals. But they build community. Their love for long-distance running makes them a team.

"He does kung fu leaps into aid stations."

More Than Marathons

What is an ultra marathon? How do ultra runners view marathons? What are different types of ultra runners?

Winter Vinecki is the youngest person to run a marathon on all seven continents. She's also the youngest person to complete a marathon in Antarctica. She was 14 years old. She's been racing since age five. Marathons aren't enough for her. She wants to compete in **ultra marathons**.

An ultra marathon, or ultra, is a long footrace. The shortest ultra is about 30 miles (48 km). Ultra runners usually run at least 50 miles (80.5 km). Most ultra runners run more than 100 miles (161 km). There's no limit to ultra distances. These races can last several days. Ultra marathons take place on roads, trails, and tracks.

Ultra runners see marathons as a **warm-up**. A warm-up is practicing before racing.

There aren't many rules for ultra marathons. Runners may take walking breaks. They may stop to drink, eat, and sleep.

There are two main types of events. Runners can cover a fixed distance. Or runners can cover the greatest possible distance within a fixed period of time.

Ultra runners prefer running in nature rather than on streets. They prefer trees to traffic.

Extreme Ultra Running: Know the Lingo

Bonking: when runners feel they can't go one more step

Cadence: number of steps taken per minute while running

Carbo-loading: eating pasta, bread, and bagels to store energy

DOMS: delayed-onset muscle soreness; discomfort that occurs 24 to 48 hours after running

Fartleks: easy runs broken up by quick sprinting bursts

Fuel: energy bars, candy, or other food to increase energy

Junk miles: short, slow runs that take place within a day after a long, harder run

LSD: long slow distance; the week's longest run

Rabbit: a runner who serves as a pacesetter during a race

Skyrunning: mountain running

Streak: running every day for a long period of time

There are different types of ultra runners. Journey runners cover long distances. They run at their own pace. **Transcontinental** runners run across countries and continents. Megarunners run in as many races as they can.

Ultra runners can set their own rules.

Inspiration

3

How did Pheidippides inspire ultra running? How did the Tarahumara inspire ultra running? Who is Miguel Vivaldo? Who is Micah True?

Pheidippides was an ancient Greek soldier. He lived in 490 BC. He ran 26 miles (42 km). He ran from the town of Marathon to Athens. He did it in 36 hours. He cried, "Nike!" This means victory. Then he died. More than 2,000 years later, the marathon became part of the first Olympics.

Spartathlon is an ultra. It's a difficult race. It partly follows Pheidippides's path. It's about 153 miles (246 km). Runners run through olive groves, steep hillsides, and rolling hills.

At night, runners climb up a mountain. They face cold temperatures. Runners face hot temperatures during the day.

The Tarahumara are Native Americans. They live in northwestern Mexico. They're famous for long-distance running. They call themselves the "running people."

The word *marathon* comes from the town of Marathon. It has Greek roots.

Spotlight Biography: Chantel "Tails" Hunt

Chantel "Tails" Hunt is a Navajo. She started running in ninth grade. She thought she'd have a "better chance of getting scholarships and being noticed." She ran for the Wings of America. It's a group of American Indians. Members are from reservations across the country. She's featured in a film called *Run to the East*. She runs on old logging roads. She zigzags through tall pine trees. She runs on packed dirt trails. Her older brother, Arvid, helped her. Running past a pit bull became part of their routine. Arvid said, "That dog on the side is the one we watch out for. We save our energy so when we come through here, we can do a speed workout for a half mile." Hunt motivated herself to finish races. She said, "I just got tired and asked myself, Why am I doing this? I don't have to. And I said, No, keep going, keep going."

They adapted to the mountain air. They can run 200 miles (322 km) over two days. They run to share news between villages. They run to transport things. They run to hunt.

They run through rough canyon country. They run on stony trails. They run in sandals or bare feet.

In 1992, a Tarahumara runner entered a 100-mile (161 km) race. He was 55 years old. He wore sandals and a **toga**. A toga is a cloth wrapped around the body. He defeated top ultra runners. The next year, another Tarahumara runner competed. He broke a record. They never ran in an ultra race again.

The Tarahumara believe humans should be in constant motion.

The Tarahumara inspired Miguel Vivaldo. Vivaldo runs to raise money for them. As a middle school student, he was winning races. He ran 84 miles (135 km) in a 24-hour event. He finished second.

Vivaldo loves competing in ultras. He said, "It was pretty exciting. I was hurting. But it wasn't a pain that hurt. It was something that felt good. I had accomplished something."

The Tarahumara also inspired Micah True. He promoted their running culture. True is known as White Horse or Caballo Blanco. He went missing. Ultra runners helped search for him. His body was found. But his death and disappearance is still a mystery.

True directed the Copper Canyon Ultra Marathon. It's a 50-mile (80.5 km) race. After his death, it was renamed the Ultra Marathon Caballo Blanco.

Ultra runners suffer from burning lungs and aching legs.

History of Ultra Marathons

4

How did ultra marathons develop? What were some of the first ultras? What are some examples of major ultras?

In 1928, Charles C. Pyle hosted the Trans-America Footrace. It started in Los Angeles. It ended in New York City. Andy Payne won. He finished in about 573 hours. He completed 3,423 miles (5,509 km) in 84 days.

The first known American ultra marathon was held by the New York Road Runners Club. It was 30 miles (48 km). It took place in 1958. Ted Corbitt won. He completed the race in about 3 hours. Corbitt is known as the father of U.S. ultra running. He won awards. He created standards. He organized ultras.

In 1974, Gordy Ainsleigh was in a horse race. His horse got hurt. So he ran the 100 miles (161 km) on foot. He finished in less than 24 hours. He inspired the Western States 100-Mile Endurance Run. It's the world's oldest and most respected race. Runners follow in Ainsleigh's footsteps.

There are many ultras. The Marathon des Sables is the most famous. It's 155 miles (249.5 km). It's in the Sahara Desert. Runners are dropped into the area. They are given supplies.

The Marathon des Sables challenges runners with extreme conditions.

They fight heat and dust storms. They clean their eyeballs at aid stations. At least three people have died.

When Extreme Is Too Extreme!

Keith Whyte has a bone condition. He suffered a back injury. Nothing stopped him from ultra running. He won the Antarctic 100-K. It's a 62.1-mile (100 km) race. Runners have to wear at least three layers of clothing. The first layer absorbs sweat. The second layer warms the body. The third layer protects runners from the wind. Runners must wear a mask, goggles, hat, and gloves. He finished in 9 hours and 26 minutes. There's constant daylight in Antarctica. So Whyte hadn't slept in three days. He fought against cold temperatures. He got frostbite. Frostbite is when body parts freeze. He almost lost his fingers. He said, "I wanted to bite my fingers just to get the feeling back." He ran against ice-cold winds. He got a bad windburn on his face. Whyte pushed himself to win. He said, "It was an amazing once-in-a-lifetime experience."

Ultra runners must train for the weather. To do the Jungle Marathon, they run on treadmills in a sauna or greenhouse.

Badwater is a 135-mile (217 km) race. It's a demanding race. Runners cross Death Valley. It's really hot. It covers three mountain ranges.

The Self-Transcendence Race is the world's longest footrace. It's 3,100 miles (4,989 km). It takes place in Queens, New York. Runners run 5,649 laps around one block. They have 52 days to complete it.

The Jungle Marathon takes place in the Amazon. Runners face dangerous animals and extreme humidity. They cross rivers. They climb mountains. It's 79 miles (127 km).

Running Records!

How have ultra runners broken records? Who is Budhia Singh? Who is Colby Wentlandt? Who is Kim Allan? Who is Cliff Young?

Budhia Singh is the world's youngest ultra marathon runner. He was born in India. He did a lot by the age of four. He ran 40 miles (64 km). He did it in seven hours and two minutes. He completed 48 marathons.

Singh was born to a poor family. His father died. His mother left him. He lived in an **orphanage**. It's a place for kids without parents. He got in trouble. He was punished. He had to run. He was still running five hours later. His talent was discovered. He trained for ultra marathons. He appeared on television. He was featured in a film. It was called *Marathon Boy*.

Colby Wentlandt was the youngest person to complete a 100-mile (161 km) race. He was 12 years old. Wentlandt said, "One reason why I like running is you can't blame anyone else for having it go wrong. It's all you, the blame

Ultra runners come in all shapes and sizes. Even young children are ultra runners.

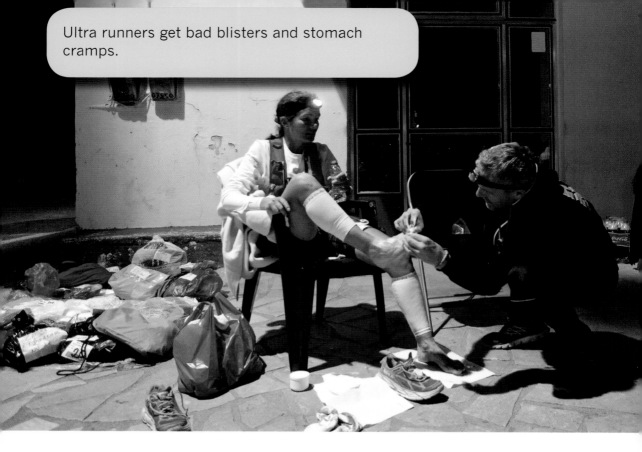

Ultra runners get bad blisters and stomach cramps.

and the accomplishment." He wants to be the youngest person to finish the Badwater race.

Kim Allan broke a world's women's record. She did the longest run without sleep. She covered about 311 miles (500.5 km). She did this in 86 hours. She said, "There's ultra runners who go out and train huge miles. That's not me. It's the beating my own mind that I like. Thinking you can't do something, then you go out and do it."

Cliff Young competed in Australia's hardest ultra. It's 544 miles (875.5 km). No one thought he'd win. He was 61 years old. He was a potato farmer. He ran slowly. But he won! He broke the record by two days. He was ahead by 10 hours.

NAILED IT!

That Happened?!?

Reza Baluchi is an Iranian American ultra runner. He's set long-distance running records. He ran from New York to Los Angeles. He ran 3,300 miles (5,311 km). He did this in 43 days. He also ran the perimeter of the United States. This means he ran around the outside border. He ran more than 11,000 miles (17,703 km). It took him six months. He wanted another challenge. He wanted to run from Florida to Bermuda. To do so, he had to run across water. He made an inflatable bubble. He spent thousands of dollars making it. He ran inside it. He hoped to run in it for the entire 1,033 miles (1,662.5 km). He only stopped to catch fish and sleep. He had protein bars, water, a navigation device, and a phone. He practiced two years for this trip. He got tired. He signaled for the Coast Guard. A helicopter picked him up. He was treated and released. He did not complete the run.

How did Young win? He trained on his farm. He chased cows. He herded sheep. He stayed awake for many nights. During the race, runners slept. Not Young. He napped for two hours. Then he ran. He didn't need as much sleep as other runners.

Most ultra runners don't run for records or prizes. They run for the challenge. They run for friendship. Robert Boyce is the president of Australia's Ultra Runners Association. He said, "You get friends for life. … It's because of the time you spend together."

Ultra runners enjoy the challenge.

Did You Know?

- Ultra runners put a lot of pressure on their toes. So they get blisters under their toenails. This turns their toenails black. Their toenails fall off! Most ultra runners don't have any toenails. Marshall Ulrich is an ultra runner. He removed all his toenails.

- Ultra runners eat every 20 to 30 minutes. They need to maintain their energy levels.

- Ed Ettinghausen is known as "The Jester." He wears a jester outfit during his races. He set a world record. He completed the most 100-mile (161 km) runs in a year. He did it in a 13-week period.

- Researchers from the University of Durham studied runners. They learned that runners who wear red clothing are more likely to win competitions.

- More than one billion pairs of running shoes are sold worldwide each year.

- The oldest person to complete a marathon was Fauja Singh. He's from India. He was 100 years old. He started racing at 89 years of age.

- Ultra runners suffer aching joints. They may have breathing problems. They hurt their knees and bones. But their biggest problem in a race is not sleeping. They are very tired after a race.

Consider This!

TAKE A POSITION! Some people think ultra running is dangerous. An ultra runner in California got lost. She was missing for three days. She didn't have food or water. Ultra runners must be safe. Most ultra runners make sure they have supplies. They carry food, water, a phone, and a navigation device. Do you think ultra running is safe or dangerous? Argue your point with reasons and evidence.

SAY WHAT? Marathons and ultra marathons have similarities and differences. Explain how they are alike and how they are different. Which one would you be interested in running and why?

THINK ABOUT IT! Long-distance running has been around for centuries. The Tarahumara run long distances. It's part of their culture. How does a tradition develop into a sport?

SEE A DIFFERENT SIDE! Some people think that children and teens are too young to do ultra running. Why do you think this is so? Research the risks and benefits of ultra running. Then consider the pros and cons for children and teens.

Learn More: Resources

PRIMARY SOURCES

Finding Traction, a documentary about ultra runner Nikki Kimball (a film by Jaime Jacobsen and Montana PBS, 2014), http://findingtractionfilm.com.

Whiting, Jim. *Ultra Running with Scott Jurek*. Hockessin, DE: Mitchell Lane Publishers, 2007.

SECONDARY SOURCES

Hayhurst, Chris. *Ultra Marathon Running*. New York: Rosen Publishing Group, 2002.

WEB SITES

American Ultrarunning Association: www.americanultra.org

International Association of Ultrarunners: www.iau-ultramarathon.org

USA Ultra Running—The Official Site of U.S. Ultra Running Teams: www.usaultrarunning.com

Glossary

aid stations (AYD STAY-shuhnz) checkpoints during a race that provide snacks, water, and first aid

arctic (AHRK-tik) extremely cold and wintry

marathon (MAR-uh-thahn) a footrace that is 26.2 miles (42 km) long

orphanage (OR-fuh-nij) a place that houses orphans or kids without parents

toga (TOH-guh) a cloth wrapped around the body

transcontinental (trans-kahn-tuh-NEN-tuhl) going across a country or continent

ultra marathons (UHL-truh MAR-uh-thahnz) footraces that are longer than a marathon

ultra runners (UHL-truh RUHN-urz) people who run longer distances than marathon runners

warm-up (WORM-uhp) a practice session before the race

Index

BOOK CHARGING CARD

Accession No. _____ Call No. _____

Author _____

Title _____

Date Loaned	Borrower's Name	Date Returned